CLIMATE CHANGE
Floods
By Bulla McIvor

Library For All Ltd.

Floods and Climate Change

A flood is what happens when excess water overflows onto land. Oceans, rivers, creeks, dams and even gutters can all flood and damage property or threaten lives.

Climate change has caused rising sea levels and more frequent deadly storms. Flooding is therefore more common and dangerous to people both on the coast and inland.

Preparing for floods is important to keep you and your community safe.

If you are caught in a flood, you should hold onto floating objects and call for help.

Traditional Signs of a Flood

Traditional, early warning signs of a flood come from nature. Wildlife, such as birds, ants, frogs and lizards, will change their behaviour when they sense dangerous weather. Some plants will also react, like closing leaves, flowering early or producing excess sap.

Birds flying erratically in big groups indicates an approaching storm.

Large numbers of ants climbing nearby trees can mean they have sensed imminent flooding or heavy rain, which often leads to floods. The ants are trying to reach higher ground to stay safe, which is something humans do, too.

DID YOU KNOW?

Frogs croaking non-stop during unusual times of the day can also mean incoming rain or massive shifts in the weather.

How Floods Are Predicted

Modern Science

With climate change impacting flood frequency, measuring rainfall is the best way to find out if one will happen. Scientists calculate how much rain occurs during a storm and, from there, tell the public whether it may turn into a flood.

Australia has a Flood Warning System to help reduce damage.

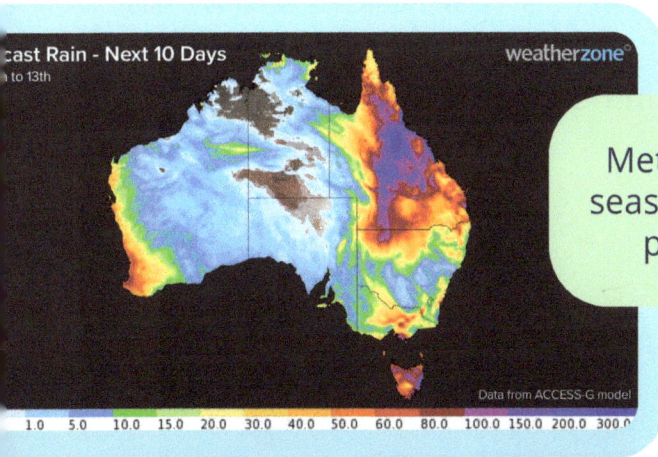

cast Rain - Next 10 Days
to 13th

weatherzone

Data from ACCESS-G model

1.0 5.0 10.0 15.0 20.0 30.0 40.0 50.0 60.0 80.0 100.0 150.0 200.0 300.0

Meteorologists use seasonal forecasts to predict floods.

Preparation Strategies
Traditional and Modern

Traditionally, the Melsonby community's preparations for floods prioritises moving to higher ground and utilising ancient rock shelters to stay safe. These shelters have helped Melsonby people through many floods over thousands of years. Teaching children using stories and songs is also a preventative measure, so they learn to take floods seriously.

Modern strategies include sandbagging or closing up the house before evacuating to higher ground. Communities often need to leave their belongings behind, and these two strategies can provide some protection for houses against the floodwater. Reducing property damage is an important step in flood preparation.

Preparation Strategies

Store extra food and clothes in high, dry places to keep them safe from floodwater.	Keep important documents, valuables and necessities up high, too.
Prepare emergency kits that include drinking water, first-aid supplies, clothes and non-perishable food.	Learn traditional navigation from Elders, so you can move safely during the floods.
Have members of the community willing to scout the water levels and weather changes.	Communication! Ensure you stay in contact with others; learn and use traditional smoke or drums, if necessary.
Have an evacuation plan within your community and practise it beforehand.	Identify evacuation points, safe zones and resources beforehand.
Give specific roles and responsibilities to those in the community, ensuring everyone is involved.	Keep tools, like ropes and tarps in a go-bag, that help people or secure shelter.
When making a shelter, make sure it is elevated and use strong materials, like wood or stone.	Pay attention to any natural indicators of floods or weather changes, like animal behaviour.

DISASTER PREPAREDNESS
CHECKLIST

- ☑ FIRST AID KIT
- ☐ FLASHLIGHT, RADIO AND SPARE BATTERI
- ☐ BLANKETS, CLOTHES AND SHOES
- ☐ TINNED AND DRIED FOOD
- ☐ EATING UTEN

11

Effects on Land and Community

There are also long-term consequences from floods. They can lead to ecological changes, including altered landforms, degraded soil quality and damaged agricultural productivity.

If a fish is lucky, floods can bring new food.

Traditionally, floods have been known to cause silt and sand to fill up the rivers. This can destroy fish populations and contaminate clean water, making food and clean water harder to find.

Response and Recovery

Modern flood response and recovery usually includes government aid: people affected by a flood are given money and shelter to help them get back on their feet; debris is removed; and repairs are organised for public spaces ruined by floodwater.

Many damaged buildings are rebuilt with additional flood resistance.

Response and Recovery in Melsonby

Within Melsonby community, Balngarrawara Rangers collaborate to help speed recovery and reassure their neighbours.

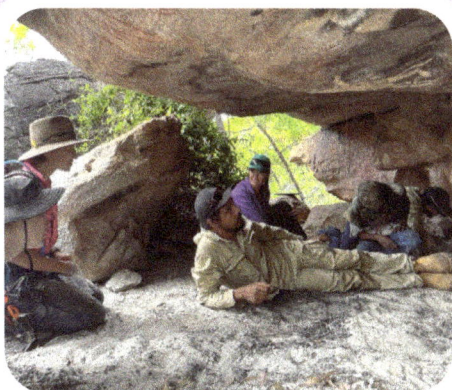

They share traditional preparation and recovery knowledge alongside modern methods, so everyone is ready.

Keeping community relationships strong is as important as rebuilding and staying safe. Land gets damaged during floods, so rebuilding includes recultivating nature and restoring ecological balance.

Cultural Impacts and Stories

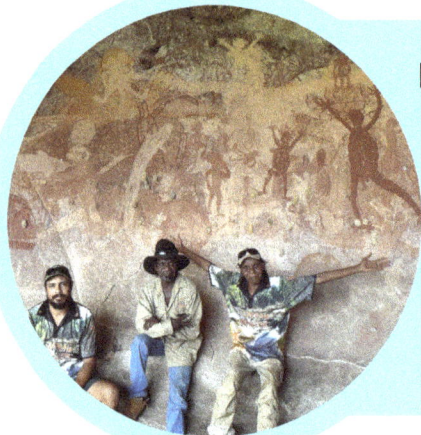

Natural disasters can also damage cultural sites. Rock art and the Bora Grounds in Melsonby are a key part of community heritage and are at risk from dangerous weather.

Sacred sites are protected during floods and rebuilt afterwards, if necessary. Smoking ceremonies are performed to clear the land of negative energies, which further bolsters community spirit.

However, if the damage is too great, some cultural sites and important history are completely wiped from existence.

Rock art and scar trees are especially vulnerable to damage from floodwaters and wind. Much traditional history is lost when a scar tree is destroyed.

Community and Environmental Resilience

 Handling the future of flooding is going to be difficult as climate change makes dangerous weather more and more common. Communication between community and their Rangers is key for building resilience and ensuring environmental stewardship.

Everyone can learn to heed natural-disaster warnings.

It is crucial that future generations know how to act during a flood.

Photo Credits

Page	Attribution
Cover	Adwo/Shutterstock.com
Pages 2–3	Wes Warren/Unsplash.com
Page 4	totajla/Shutterstock.com
Page 5	Cavan-Images/Shutterstock.com
Page 6	Image courtesy of the Queensland Indigenous Land and Sea Ranger Program.
Page 7	Image courtsey of Australian Institute for Disaster Resilience.
Page 7	Image courtsey of Weatherzone.
Page 9 (background)	Image courtesy of the Queensland Indigenous Land and Sea Ranger Program.
Page 9 (bottom)	Silken Photography/Shutterstock.com
Page 11 (above)	Speedshutter Photography/Shutterstock.com
Page 11 (below)	lemono/Shutterstock.com
Page 12-13	Cloudcatcher Media/Shutterstock.com
Page 14	Maythee Voran/Shutterstock.com
Page 15 (both)	Image courtesy of the Queensland Indigenous Land and Sea Ranger Program.
Page 16 (both)	Image courtesy of the Queensland Indigenous Land and Sea Ranger Program.
Page 17	Image courtesy of the Queensland Indigenous Land and Sea Ranger Program.
Page 18-19 (background)	© Library For All
Page 19	Image courtesy of the Queensland Indigenous Land and Sea Ranger Program.

You can use these questions to talk about this book with your family, friends and teachers.

What did you learn from this book?

Describe this book in one word. Funny? Scary? Colourful? Interesting?

How did this book make you feel when you finished reading it?

What was your favourite part of this book?

Queensland Indigenous Land and Sea Ranger Program

The Queensland Indigenous Land and Sea Ranger Program collaborates with First Nations communities to protect and care for land and sea Country. With over 200 rangers, the program shares cultural knowledge, engages in community education, and leads youth programs like the Junior Ranger initiative, fostering a strong connection to Country and Culture.

Bulla is a Balnggarrawarra Ranger from the Melsonby community.

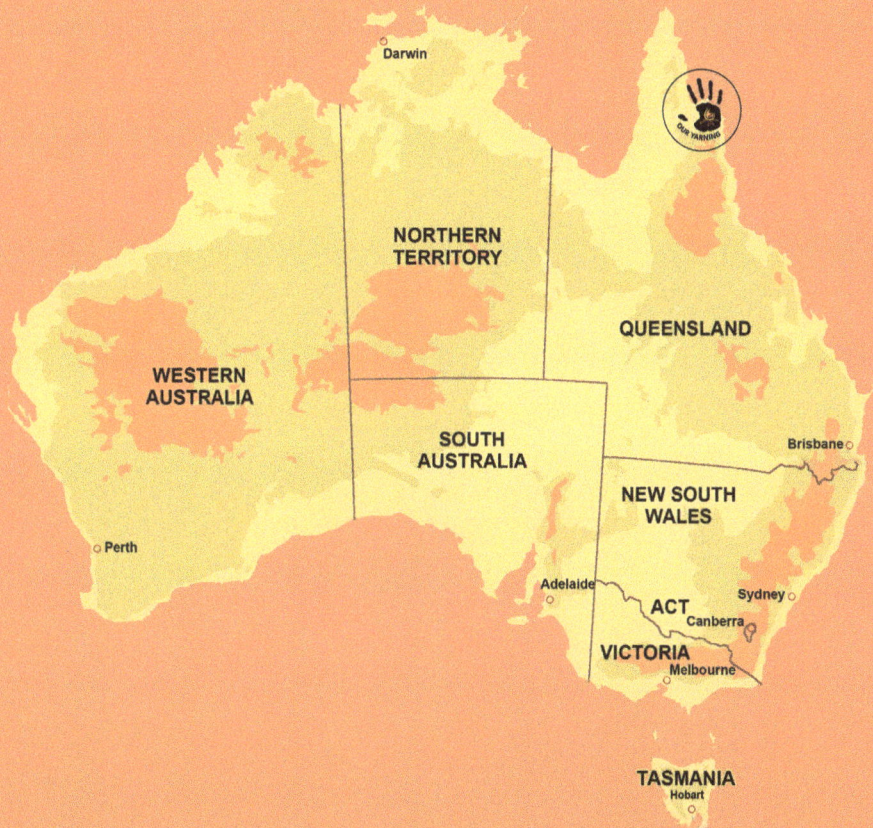

Darwin

NORTHERN
TERRITORY

QUEENSLAND

WESTERN
AUSTRALIA

SOUTH
AUSTRALIA

Brisbane

NEW SOUTH
WALES

Perth

Adelaide

ACT
Canberra

Sydney

VICTORIA
Melbourne

TASMANIA
Hobart

Our Yarning

The Our Yarning collection aligns with the Australian Curriculum through the Cross-Curriculum Priorities — Aboriginal and Torres Strait Islander Histories and Cultures. The collection provides an authentic opportunity for learning and embedding Aboriginal and Torres Strait Islander perspectives because it is written by Aboriginal and Torres Strait Islander people.

We know that children learn better, and enjoy reading more, when they see themselves in the stories, characters and illustrations of the books they read.

To download the app, visit the Google Play Store or Apple Store and search 'Our Yarning'.

libraryforall.org

You're reading Upper Primary

Learner – Beginner readers
Start your reading journey with short words, big ideas and plenty of pictures.

Level 1 – Rising readers
Raise your reading level with more words, simple sentences and exciting images.

Level 2 – Eager readers
Enjoy your reading time with familiar words, but complex sentences.

Level 3 – Progressing readers
Develop your reading skills with creative stories and some challenging vocabulary.

Level 4 – Fluent readers
Step up your reading skills with playful narratives, new words and fun facts.

Middle Primary – Curious readers
Discover your world through science and stories.

Upper Primary – Adventurous readers
Explore your world through science and stories.

Library For All is an Australian not for profit organisation with a mission to make knowledge accessible to all via an innovative digital library solution.
Visit us at libraryforall.org

Climate Change: Floods

First published 2024

Published by Library For All Ltd
Email: info@libraryforall.org
URL: libraryforall.org

This project was delivered with the support of QBE under the Community Ready partnership.

Community Ready

This book was made possible with the support of the Queensland Indigenous Land and Sea Ranger Program to support educational outcomes for children in Australia by learning from Indigenous knowledge and stewardship of Country. To learn more, visit https://www.qld.gov.au/environment/plants-animals/conservation/community/land-sea-rangers/locations.

Our Yarning logo design by Jason Lee, Bidjipidji Art

Climate Change: Floods
McIvor, Bulla
ISBN: 978-1-923207-37-0
SKU04431

www.ingramcontent.com/pod-product-compliance
Lightning Source LLC
Chambersburg PA
CBHW042343040426
42448CB00019B/3389